Cutest Puppies Ever!

QEB

Quarto is the authority on a wide range of topics.

Quarto educates, entertains and enriches the lives of our readers—enthusiasts and lovers of hands-on living.

www.quartoknows.com

Copyright © QEB Publishing, Inc. 2016

First published in the United States in 2016
by QEB Publishing, Inc.
Part of The Quarto Group
6 Orchard
Lake Forest, CA 92630

Publisher: Maxime Boucknooghe
Design: Tracy Killick Art Direction & Design
Editorial Director: Victoria Garrard
Art Director: Miranda Snow

A CIP record for this book is available from the Library of Congress.

ISBN 978 1 68297 069 0

Printed in China

Contents

Which is the cutest of them all?
Read on and find out!

Afghan Hound

Long, silky fur, floppy ears, big feet, and a long nose give an Afghan hound pup a comical look.

But don't be fooled—this proud, ancient breed is a super-fast runner and graceful jumper.

She has a silly side as well, though…she's great at sneaking up and stealing snacks from right under your nose!

Akita

How cute is this super-cuddly fluffball!? Meet the akita, a brave, reliable guard dog from Japan, bred with thick fur for snowy weather.

As well as being cute, an akita puppy is calm, quiet, and laid-back. Instead of barking or whimpering, she'll just curl up for a snooze!

Alaskan Malamute

This cute fluffy pup looks a lot like a wolf— and he *is* a lot like a wolf!

Bred for cold, snowy places, malamutes love exercise. They need to run around outdoors, or else they'll go crazy, howl, chew up your couch, or raid the trash can!

Despite all this, though, they're friendly, loyal pets.

American Bulldog

You can tell a bulldog by its wide head, short muzzle, and big mouth. In puppy form, they look super-sweet.

American bulldogs were bred to be strong, outdoor farm dogs, so they need a LOT of exercise.

Their puppies are noisy, playful, funny, and jumpy— and drool quite a lot too! Eww!

American Staffordshire Terrier

Even as a puppy, the American Staffordshire terrier is a strong, brave dog.

People are sometimes scared of them because of their big teeth. But these puppies are among the most lovable, easygoing, good-natured doggies you could meet.

They'll bounce everywhere, jump up to greet you, and give you a big slobbery kiss!

Basset Hound

With their big feet, long floppy ears, and pleading eyes, basset hound puppies are sweet, goofy, and so cute!

These friendly, happy pups have an amazing sense of smell, and love to sniff things out.

They also adore people, food, and lazing around and snoozing whenever they can.

Beagle

Beagle puppies are a bit of a handful. They're always up to mischief—chewing things, raiding the kitchen for food, or running away to follow an interesting scent.

It's lucky they're also funny, friendly, and incredibly cute! A beagle pup's big, brown eyes could make you forgive them for anything.

Bearded Collie

If you want a puppy who never stops bouncing around, a bearded collie is for you!

This pup gets his name from his silky-soft, waterproof coat, and his endless excitement and jumpy playfulness is known as the "Beardie bounce".

He's a waggy-tailed, loyal, loving, happy-go-lucky cutie who makes a fabulously fun pet.

Bernese Mountain Dog

This pup is strong and smart, with a super-sweet nature.

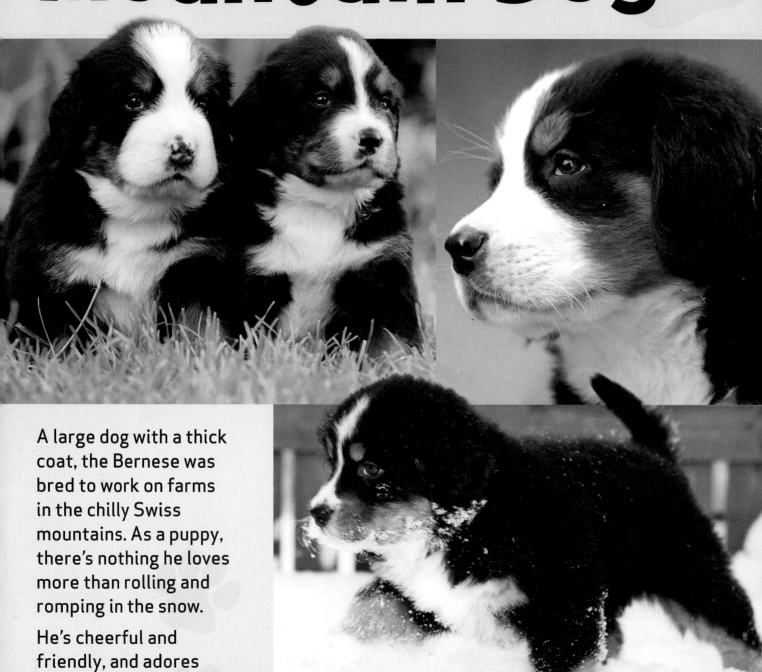

A large dog with a thick coat, the Bernese was bred to work on farms in the chilly Swiss mountains. As a puppy, there's nothing he loves more than rolling and romping in the snow.

He's cheerful and friendly, and adores children.

Bichon Frise

Tiny, cuddly, soft, and fluffy, a bichon frise is the ultimate adorable pup.

He's calm, loves children, and always wants to interact.

In fact, bichons are so sweet, caring, and sensitive, they often work as therapy dogs. They are taken into hospitals or nursing homes to snuggle with the patients and cheer them up.

Border Collie

This puppy seems to be looking right into your soul—and maybe he is!

Highly intelligent, border collies develop a close bond with humans. Some owners say their dogs can even read their minds!

Border collies were bred to round up sheep, and they love to keep busy, as working dogs or by learning tricks.

Borzoi

Sweet, sensible, and laid back—that's a borzoi puppy. Until, that is, she sees something to chase, and she zooms off at incredible speed!

In Russia, where this breed comes from, the name "Borzoi" means "fast".

Borzoi pups are also affectionate, and love to cuddle in your lap—even though they're a bit too big!

Cavalier King Charles Spaniel

Just imagine stroking this puppy's long, soft, silky ears!

Gentle and friendly, a Cavalier King Charles spaniel puppy is the ultimate cuddly companion.

He loves curling up on your lap for some attention. But he's also a fast runner, and will chase anything—balls, cats, squirrels, even birds and butterflies!

Chihuahua

The Chihuahua is the world's smallest dog, so imagine how teeny and cute its puppies are!

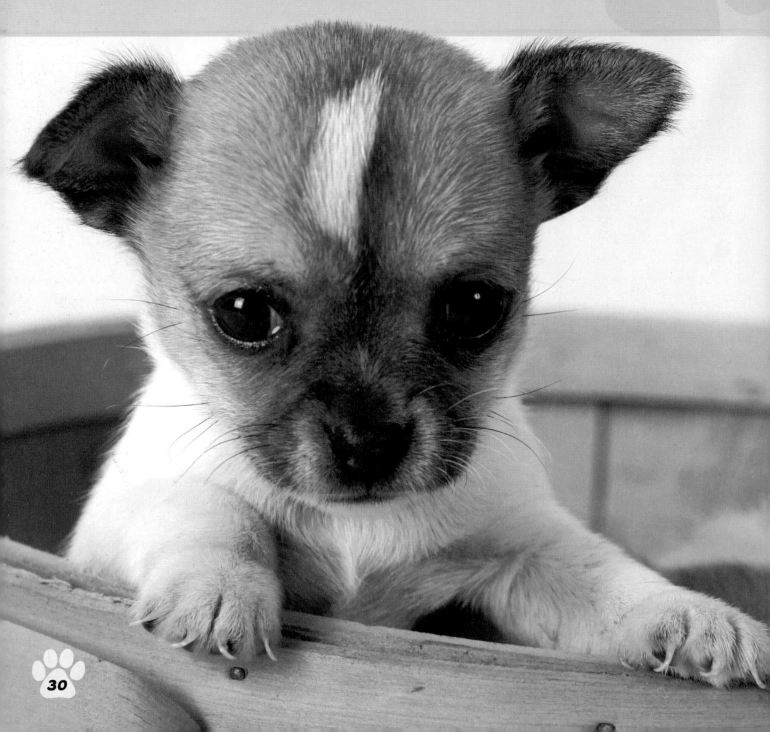

They make up for it, though, with a big personality—they're smart, bold, curious, comical, and quirky.

They don't need much exercise, and prefer being carried in a handbag or snuggling in a cozy spot.

Chinese Crested Dog

This funny-looking pup is also known as a powder puff dog—how cute is that?

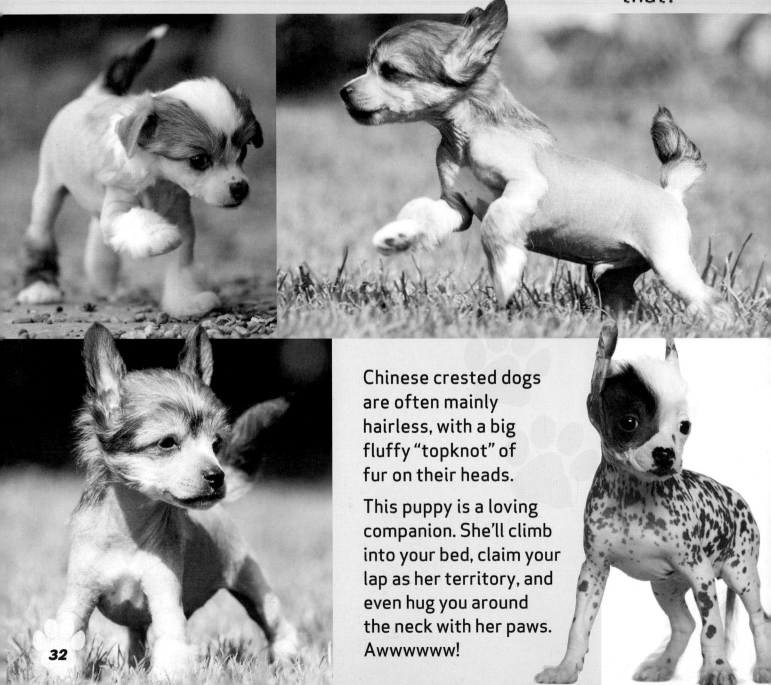

Chinese crested dogs are often mainly hairless, with a big fluffy "topknot" of fur on their heads.

This puppy is a loving companion. She'll climb into your bed, claim your lap as her territory, and even hug you around the neck with her paws. Awwwwww!

Chow Chow

Could THIS be the cutest puppy ever? With her squishy face, crumpled ears, and slightly grumpy expression, a chow chow puppy just makes your heart melt!

Chows are from China, where they are known as "puffy lion dogs". They have an unusual blue-black tongue, and are good at learning tricks.

Cockapoo

Just try saying "No!" to this gorgeous little face. You couldn't, could you?

Few puppies are as over-the-top cute, friendly, and loving as a cockapoo—a cross between a poodle and a cocker spaniel.

Once she's made friends with you, a cockapoo pup will never want to leave your side.

Corgi

With his short stubby legs, eager face, and fluffy fur, a corgi pup is like a real live plush doggy toy!

Corgis aren't just cute though—
they are reliable, brave dogs who
like to guard their family home.

They love children, but watch
out: a corgi pup can sometimes
be naughty and give you a nip!

Dachshund

The dachshund is also known as the sausage dog, and that's pretty cute!

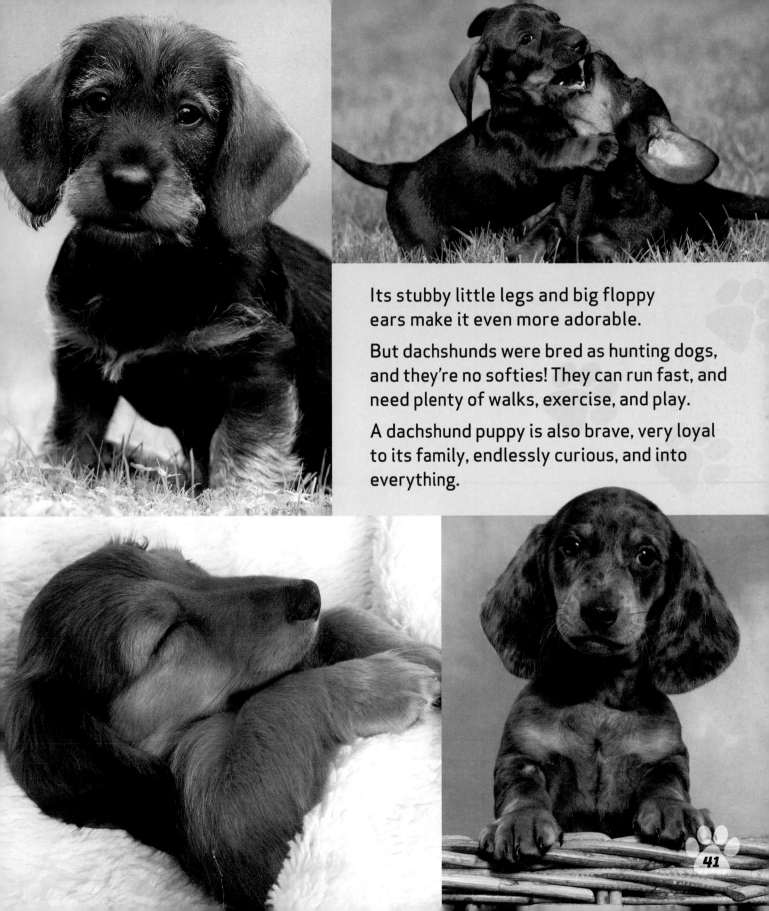

Its stubby little legs and big floppy ears make it even more adorable.

But dachshunds were bred as hunting dogs, and they're no softies! They can run fast, and need plenty of walks, exercise, and play.

A dachshund puppy is also brave, very loyal to its family, endlessly curious, and into everything.

Dalmatian

Famous for his gorgeous spotted coat,
this is a puppy with a BIG personality.

Dalmatian pups have endless high-speed energy, and the waggiest tails ever! They just love to leap all over you, and they adore children and families.

They're bouncy, boisterous, and sometimes a bit of a handful!

Doberman Pinscher

Look at this puppy's alert, intelligent eyes!

Even as a little pup, she's on the lookout, eager to explore, play, and protect her human family.

Doberman pinschers learn easily, and can become wonderful guard dogs or police dogs. But they're not as scary as some people think—they're just big softies who are fiercely loyal!

German Shepherd

So sweet and fluffy now, this gorgeous puppy will grow into a confident, brave, and devoted dog.

The German shepherd is one of the most popular pet dogs of all. These pups love to run, jump, fetch, and play.

They're smart and make great police dogs, guard dogs, sniffer dogs, guide dogs, or rescue dogs.

Golden Retriever

This golden retriever pup is just like a snuggly, cuddly, cute little teddy bear!

These doggies make great family pets. They're sweet, friendly, happy, tail-waggy bundles of joy, who love to play with and please their owners.

Even when they grow up, they keep their puppy attitude—bouncy, silly, and fun!

Great Dane

Dogs don't come much bigger than a Great Dane. Even as a puppy, he's a giant with a loud bark.

These pups can be clumsy and messy, and will knock over and squash most of the stuff in your house as they leap around wagging their tails!

But underneath, they are gentle, easygoing, and loving.

Greyhound

Greyhounds are FAST runners. Even the puppies have long legs and sleek bodies, and love chasing anything they can.

But once they've had a good run, greyhound pups are calm, sweet, and gentle.

A greyhound's short hair means it can get chilly. So if it's cold, get your greyhound pup a cozy coat!

Havanese

With his soft silky coat, bright eyes, and floppy ears, a Havanese is just so loveable!

Small, snuggly and cuddly, this puppy needs to be close to people. Don't leave him alone for long —he'll miss you too much! Awwww!

Havanese pups are also playful, curious, and smart, and great at learning tricks.

Irish Setter

An Irish setter puppy is the comedy clown of the dog world. She's excitable, silly, nosy, and full of love and affection.

She's also adorable to stroke and cuddle, with her silky soft, reddish fur and floppy ears.

Though a jumpy and excitable puppy, she'll grow up to become a proud, brave, and loyal pet.

Irish Wolfhound

An Irish wolfhound puppy is a big, lovable buffoon with a funny face and incredibly cute, pleading eyes.

These sweet, gentle dogs have very long legs, and as puppies, they're often adorably clumsy and goofy. They also need lots of strokes and hugs.

They don't make good guard dogs though—they're too sweet!

59

Jack Russell

This puppy is bright, bouncy, brave, smart, and stubborn, and seems to have endless energy.

He loves to chase things, catch balls, dig holes, and run and play. He needs LOTS of affection and entertainment—but he'll reward you with loads of fun, love, and loyalty.

Komondor

Where am I!? With a straggly woolly coat that often grows over his eyes, a cute Komondor puppy looks like a hyperactive mop running around on four legs.

But this shaggy Hungarian breed is tougher than he looks.

He'll grow into a big, strong (but still very mop-like!) guard dog, who's fiercely protective of his family.

Labrador Retriever

The Labrador retriever is a friendly, playful breed—and as a bouncy, cuddly puppy, she's even more fun!

Labrador puppies just love rolling around, play-fighting and chasing things. They have warm, open faces and big, adoring eyes.

Labradors were bred to retrieve (or fetch) things from water, so they like getting wet, too.

Miniature Schnauzer

What could be more adorable than a tiny puppy with a big beard and mustache!?

Miniature schnauzers are funny, friendly, feisty puppies, with a serious fluffiness factor. They're always over the moon to see you, and make you laugh by chasing things and trying to get your attention. Just look at these cuties!

Newfoundland

Newfoundland dogs are big—VERY big! So a Newfie puppy can cause chaos as she bounces and leaps around. CRASH!

However, these pups make great pets, as they are kind, sweet-natured, and always gentle.

Newfoundlands were bred to help fishermen in the water, so they LOVE swimming—and even have webbed toes!

Old English Sheepdog

Look at this pup's face—sweet, gentle, and just a bit mischievous!

Old English sheepdog puppies are energetic and need exercise and space.

They'll leap all over you, dribble, get covered in twigs, and track mud across the floor.

To make up for it, they're big, friendly softies who'll be loyal to you forever.

Papillon

This breed is named the "Papillon," meaning butterfly, thanks to its big, beautiful, butterfly-shaped ears.

Papillon puppies are bright, friendly, and fast learners, and love playing games with their owners.

They're so small, sweet, and well-behaved, this is the kind of pup you might see a movie star carrying in her handbag!

Pomeranian

With a gorgeous foxy face, fluffy fur, and huge eyes, a Pomeranian or "pom-pom" puppy is super-cute!

Pom-pom pups are friendly, outgoing, smart, and curious. They explore everything, and they're so watchful and alert that nothing gets past them.

Though they're little, poms are proud and confident, and love to be "top dog".

Poodle

People often think of poodles as fluffy, pretty, and cute, with their soft curly coats and sweet eyes. And they certainly are!

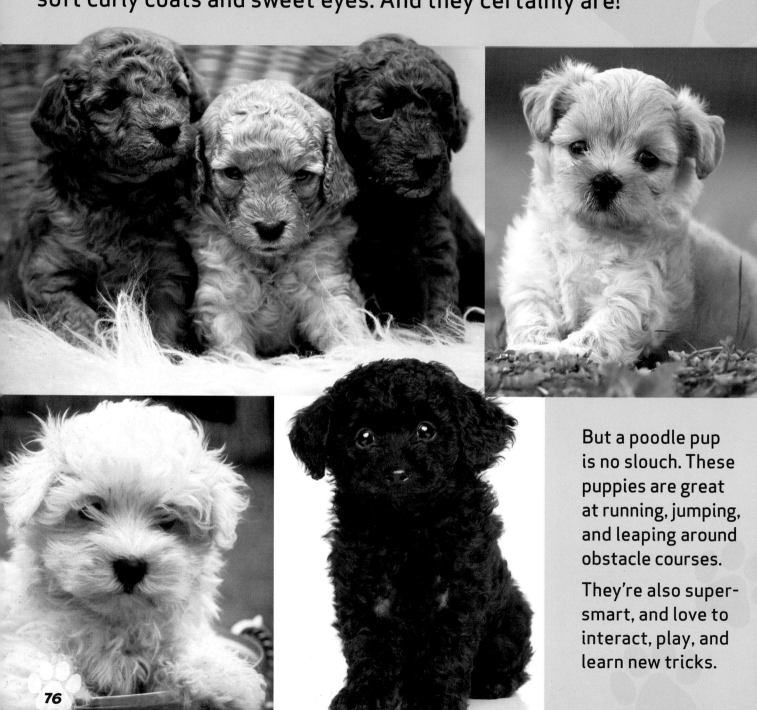

But a poodle pup is no slouch. These puppies are great at running, jumping, and leaping around obstacle courses.

They're also super-smart, and love to interact, play, and learn new tricks.

Pug

A funny little pug puppy is unlike any other dog. With his squashed-looking, wrinkly face and huge, wide-apart eyes, you could say he's kind of ugly—but in a *reeaally* cute way!

Pugs have a great sense of humor, and love to show off and get into trouble.

Puli

This tangled ball of woolly tassels has springs hidden in her feet!

Puli pups are amazingly acrobatic, and wonderful at jumping. They are also curious, playful, mischievous, and bossy, and will try to trick humans into doing what they want.

Own a Puli, and she'll wrap you around her little paw!

Rhodesian Ridgeback

She looks cute, but a Rhodesian ridgeback puppy is one tough cookie.

These dogs were bred to hunt LIONS in Africa, and they're big, brave, fast, and strong.

As puppies, they're also bursting with energy, jumpy, bouncy, and crazy!

Their name comes from a strip of fur on their backs that grows in the "wrong" direction.

Rottweiler

A Rottweiler is a big, strong, loud dog, and as a puppy he's full of energy and excitement.

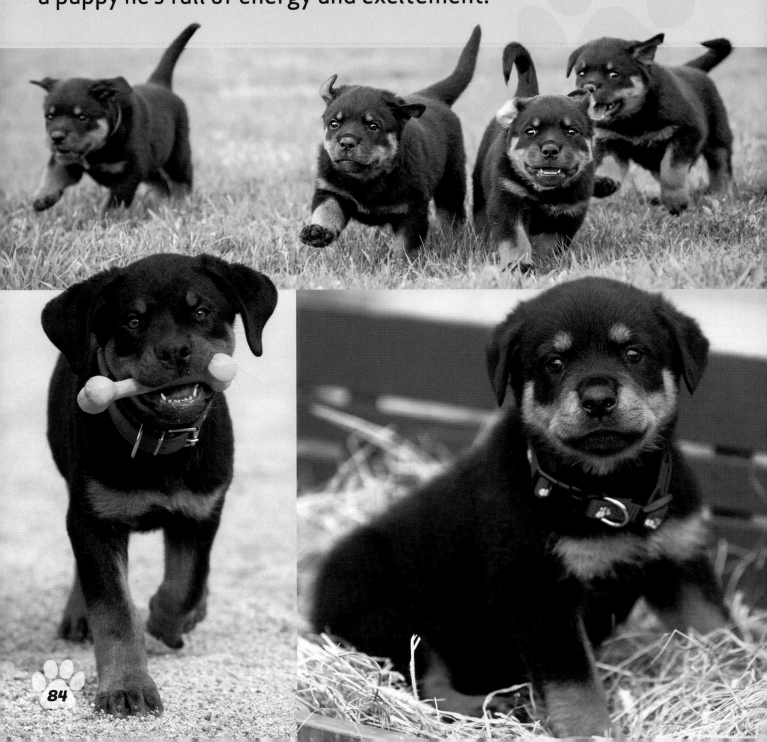

He's always jumping up, slobbering, and romping around, and will chase cats and smaller dogs if he gets a chance.

With training, though, he'll grow into a loyal, loving pet who adores his family.

Shar-Pei

As soon as you see this bundle of wrinkly fur, you just want to stroke and snuggle him!

The Chinese shar-pei is prized for his unusual looks—baggy skin, tiny ears, a curly tail, and a big head that's said to look like a hippo's! They make calm, loving, chilled-out puppies.

Shih Tzu

The shih tzu was bred to be a cuddly companion, and her impossibly cute face would make anyone want to stroke and pet her.

Her name means "lion dog", but she's not fierce at all! This happy, bright-eyed puppy only wants to make friends, lie on laps, or snuggle up in a cozy bed.

Vizsla

You can see in this puppy's big, wise eyes just how smart and thoughtful he is.

A Vizsla pup is quick to learn, with a great sense of smell—they often become working sniffer dogs.

But what they want most is to be around people, and to be stroked, petted, and loved. Awwwww!

Weimaraner

With their sleek gray coats and gorgeous blue or golden eyes, Weimaraners are beautiful puppies.

But beware—they're into everything! They'll chew up your shoes, chase cats, and destroy whole couches.

They'll also follow you around like a shadow, as they can't get enough of being walked, stroked, and hugged!

Yorkshire Terrier

A Yorkshire terrier puppy is a little cutie—and she knows it! She's tiny, but stubborn, and feisty with a big personality.

She likes to think she's the boss of the house, barking when visitors arrive, and demanding strokes and hugs.

With her silky long fur and appealing eyes, a "Yorkie" is just irresistible.

Picture acknowledgments

123RF Ermolaev Alexander 14, 15 below right; Mikkel Bigandt 73 centre left; Christopher Howey 17 below right; Cris Kelly 44 below right; Saranya Loisamut 99 below right; Kimberly Madson 37 above right; Guy Sagi 51 above left; Andrey Starostin 31 below left; Zuzana Tillerova 19; Evgeniy Zakharov 24 above left. Alamy blickwinkel/Schmidt-Roeger 5; Katrina Brown 8 above right; Farlap 9; Vanessa Grossemy 7 above left, 7 above right, 18 below left, 21, 56 below left, 86 below left; H. Mark Weidman Photography 49 above left; ImageBroker 53 above right; imageBROKER/Ariane Lohmar 79 below left; imageBROKER/Alessandra Sarti 78, 92; Juniors Bildarchiv GmbH 16, 59, 68 below right, 81 below, 87; Juniors Bildarchiv GmbH/A. Joswig 91 above right; Juniors Bildarchiv GmbH/M. Wegler 81 above right; Juniors Bildarchiv GmbH/T. Schaefer 67 below left; Life on white 35 below right; limitedqstock 64 below right; MIXA 38; Kseniya Ragozina 63 above; Kelley Stanley/Stockimo 42; Tierfotoagentur/J. Hutfluss 10 below left, 29 above, 56 above right; Tierfotoagentur/K. Luehrs 28; Tierfotoagentur/R. Richter 6 above left, 10 above left, 10 above right, 46 above right; Petra Wegner 91 above left; WILDLIFE GmbH 93 below; Jim Zuckerman 34. Dreamstime 8213profoto 43 above left; Suphatthra China 31 above right; Waldemar Dabrowski 60 above left; Dehlodi1 93 above left; Tatyana Gladskikh 60 above right; Klaugab 91 below right; Kutizoltan 49 below right; Sergey Lavrentev 73 above left, 73 above right, 73 below right; Lunja87 81 above left; Mdorottya 55 above left; Mellbee80 43 below right; Onetouchspark 4 above left; Photographerlondon 63 below left; Photowitch 22 above left; Marta Pospisilova

24 below left; Rebius 56 above left; Fesus Robert 80; Richard Thomas 37 below left; Zuzana Tillerova 18 above, 61; Tkatsai 82; Anna Utekhina 63 above right; Anke Van Wyk 31 below right; Nopporn Wijakamatee 17 above left; Xalanx 40. FLPA ImageBROKER 65; ImageBROKER/Adam Friedhelm 41 above left; Tierfotoagentur/Ivonne Felgenhauer 41 above right; Tierfotoagentur/Dana Geithner 64 above right; Tierfotoagentur/Jeanette Hutfluss 41 below right. Getty Images Kerstin Meyer 69; Narelle Sartain, alternate take photography AU 53 left; Wild Horse Photography 25. iStockphoto adamkaz 37 below right; Jonathan Brizendine 29 below left; ClarityPhotography 35 below left; fotojagodka 7 below; igartist 53 below right; JStaley401 68 below left; kirendia 37 above left; lariko3 74 below left; Sergey Lavrentev 12 above left; LiuMeiLi 8 below left; MarinaMassel 76 above left; Pekic 20 left; Philartphace 70; stahkmedia 36; Stefanofiorentino 76 below left; Lisa Thornberg 95 below; tsik 32 above left; Wavetop 57; Zuzule 18 below right. REX Shutterstock imageBROKER 43 above right; Sunset 71 below. Shutterstock Adya 17 below left; alekuwka 79 below right; Morten Normann Almeland 74 above right; anetapics 17 above right, 95 above left; Mila Atkovska 64 below left; beltsazar 2-3; Mikkel Bigandt 48 below left, 49 above right, 72; Sergey Bogdanov 8 top left; Canon Boy 13; Andraz Cerar 22 right; cynoclub 52; Waldemar Dabrowski 26 above left; Cheryl E. Davis 94; dezi 60 below right; DragoNika 22 below left, 93 above right; nancy dressel 83 below left, 83 below right; Ermolaev Alexander 39 below right; Ezzolo 79 above right; Natalia Fadosova 24 right; Fedora_M 60 below left; Hugo Felix 46

below right; Fotyma 29 below right; Stephanie Frey 67 above left; gorillaimages 95 above right; Kate Grishakova 71 above right; Hannamariah 41 below left; Anna Hoychuk 31 above left; Sandra Huber 55 above right, 55 below right; hvoya 96; Eric Isselee 32 below right, 86 above; Ammit Jack 84 below left; Jagodka 67 below right, 76 below right; Jarry 32 above right, 32 below left; JLSnader 84 below right; JStaley401 68 above right; Aneta Jungerova 12 right; Andrey Khusnutdinov 68 above left; Rita Kochmarjova 1, 12 below left, 39 above left, 39 above right, 47, 58 left, 75, 84 above, 85; Alexey Kozhemyakin 77; Liliya Kulianionak 35 above, 54, Kurt M 64 above left; Sergey Lavrentev 74 above left; Lenkadan 33, 51 right; Little Moon 11; Saranya Loi 88 below left; Malivan_Iuliia 73 below left; Lurin 46 above left; MaraZe 66, 67 above right; Dorottya Mathe 55 below left; Mark McElroy 20 above right, 20 right; Katho Menden 48; Evan Meyer 71 above left; Einar Muoni 26 below; Nagel Photography 89; Nico Muller Art 56 below right; otsphoto 4 above right, 4 below, 83 above left, 83 above right, 95 below left; PCHT 76 below right; Steve Pepple 30; PHOTOCREO/Michal Bednarek 26 above right; Photohunter 58 below right; PozitivStudija 44 left, 44 above right, 45; Rabyesang 88 above; Robynrg 15 below left; Guy J. Sagi 50; Julija Sapic 86 below left; sima 6 right; spartasibe 79 above left; Trybex 6 below left; Zuzana Uhlikova 27; Anna Utekhina 62; Julie Vader 39 below left; Vivienstock 51 below left; WilleeCole Photography 15 above; Dora Zett 23, 43 below left; Vera Zinkova 46 below left; Zuzule 8 below right, 15 centre right, 58 above right, 90, 91 below left.